Boffin Boy
Set Two
Workbook One

By David Orme

Accompanies the Boffin Boy reading books

- **Boffin Boy and the Forest of the Ninja**
- **Boffin Boy and the Ice Caves of Pluto**
- **Boffin Boy and the Deadly Swarm.**

Ransom

Boffin Boy Set Two Workbook One
by David Orme

Illustrated by Peter Richardson

Published by Ransom Publishing Ltd.
51 Southgate Street, Winchester Hants. SO23 9EH UK
www.ransom.co.uk

ISBN 978 184167 707 1
First published in 2008

A CIP catalogue record of this book is available from the British Library.

Design and layout: www.macwiz.co.uk

Find out more about Boffin Boy at www.ransom.co.uk

Contents

Introduction 4

Boffin Boy and the Forest of the Ninja
Teacher's Notes 5
Worksheet 1 - The Newspaper Story 7
Worksheet 2 - Opinions: Is Wu Pee a Crook? 8
Worksheet 3 - Boffin Boy's Plan 9
Worksheet 4 - Wu Pee's Forest of the Ninja Quiz 10
Worksheet 5 - Anagrams 11
Worksheet 6 - Romeo and Juliet 12
Worksheet 7 - Secrets of the Wizards 13
Worksheet 8 - How Red Wolf Escaped 14

Boffin Boy and the Ice Caves of Pluto
Teacher's Notes 15
Worksheet 1 - Snugbite's Story 17
Worksheet 2 - Not Getting Lost 18
Worksheet 3 - Why Isn't Pluto a Planet? 19
Worksheet 4 - Wu Pee's Quiz 20
Worksheet 5 - Glossary 21
Worksheet 6 - Boffin Boy's Door-opening Twiddly Thing 22
Worksheet 7 - Word Mazes 23
Worksheet 8 - Planning Another Adventure 24

Boffin Boy and the Deadly Swarm
Teacher's Notes 25
Worksheet 1 - TV Report 27
Worksheet 2 - Retelling the Story 28
Worksheet 3 - Killer Bugs Website 29
Worksheet 4 - Word Code 30
Worksheet 5 - The Corpse's Story 31
Worksheet 6 - A Poster 32
Worksheet 7 - Bubbles 33
Worksheet 8 - Wu Pee to the Rescue 34

Picture Resource Pages
Teacher's Notes 35
Resource Pages 36

Introduction

The purpose of this material is to provide opportunities to check pupils' understanding of the Boffin Boy stories and to provide structures to encourage writing in a range of forms.

Pupils working at the reading level assumed by these books frequently have a mis-match between their experiential oral skills and their skills in reading and writing. The Boffin Boy stories and support materials are intended to be:

- appealing and engaging, particularly to those who may be otherwise reluctant to read, but appropriate as a fun read for all pupils;
- highly visual, with minimum text in the stories and minimum rubric on the worksheets;
- age appropriate;
- achievable; and
- appropriately challenging.

This Workbook covers three of the Boffin Boy titles: *The Forest of the Ninja*, *The Ice Caves of Pluto* and *The Deadly Swarm*. There are eight worksheets for each title, plus five sheets of artwork resources that pupils can use in various ways, including designing their own Boffin Boy graphic novels. Further ideas for these are provided in the teacher's notes. The worksheets have a literacy focus, but include a range of lighter, fun activities such as word searches and code-breaking. The sheets are introduced by a character from the story and, in keeping with the stories, are slightly more wacky and offbeat than the traditional literacy worksheet!

Each sheet is fully supported by teacher's notes. For these pupils it is essential that the work on the sheets is prepared as a class or group exercise, and suggestions for this are provided (suggestions include oral work and shared writing). Simply handing out the sheets, perhaps as a homework exercise, is unlikely to be successful.

Worksheet 1 – The Newspaper Story

Task:

Writing a newspaper account explaining why Wu Pee is a crook.

Support:

Ensure that pupils are familiar with the conventions of newspaper journalism, e.g. the use of indirect speech and of sub-headlines.

Work together to compile the evidence against Wu Pee, based upon what is contained in the story.

Discuss what else might be included in a newspaper - e.g. interviews, background information, comment from the newspaper itself.

Include in the Word box any further words arising out of the discussion.

Extension:

Write the newspaper report that might appear at the end of the story - i.e. when Wu Pee's full story is revealed.

Worksheet 2 – Opinions: Is Wu Pee a Crook?

Task:

To write two opposing opinions.

Support:

The tasks ask pupils to write the opinions of Chief Hancuff, who thinks Wu Pee is a crook, and those of Boffin Boy, who is sure that Wu Pee isn't.

For each one, work together to assemble key facts to support each view. Police Chief Hancuff will work from the evidence he has received, while Boffin Boy will focus on Wu Pee's previous good record.

The Boffin Boy opinion could be written as a response to the comments of Police Chief Hancuff.

Extension:

Write a third opinion, namely what Red Wolf thinks about Wu Pee. (This opinion could be given at different points in the story, as Red Wolf's opinion of whether Wu Pee is a crook changes.)

Worksheet 3 – Boffin Boy's Plan

Task:

To write a piece of explanatory text. Boffin Boy explains to his mum how he is going to track down Red Wolf.

Support:

Pupils will need to provide additional information beyond that supplied in the story. For example, does Boffin Boy have any idea what he is actually going to do when he does find Red Wolf and Wu Pee? Has he told Police Chief Hancuff what he is doing? Some of these concerns could be raised by Mum in her reply to Boffin Boy.

Extension:

Boffin Boy and Wu Pee are safe in the end, but the plan could have been better! Extend the writing with an explanation from Boffin Boy of what went wrong and how he could have made the plan better.

Worksheet 4 – Wu Pee's Forest of the Ninja Quiz

Task:

To answer comprehension questions based on the text.

Support:

A straightforward comprehension activity, in a quiz format. For less able pupils, this could be an oral rather than a written activity, perhaps involving teams.

Extension:

Ask pupils to devise further questions, based on the text, to extend the quiz.

Worksheet 5 – Anagrams

Task:

Solving anagrams.

Support:

Pupils can find anagrams difficult. Additional support might therefore be appropriate – e.g. writing out the anagram and cutting it up, so that pupils can physically rearrange the letters. Note that the words all begin with capital letters, providing an additional clue.

Extension:

Pupils could produce their own anagrams to challenge others. This could be an ICT exercise: there is a range of anagram creating and solving resources to be found on the Internet (search for 'anagram').

Worksheet 6 – Romeo and Juliet

Task:

Provide an outline of the story of Romeo and Juliet by William Shakespeare.

Support:

It is not anticipated that pupils will necessarily have knowledge of the Shakespeare play. The outline supplied on the sheet should be sufficient for pupils to make informed guesses about the sequence of events. These guesses could form a discussion activity.

Extension:

Ask pupils to plan other stories, using the death pill idea as a key element.

Worksheet 7 – Secrets of the Wizards

Task:

To come up with 'secrets' equally as ludicrous as the one in the story.

Support:

This is a good activity for group discussion, with groups presenting their ideas to the class.

Extension:

(ICT opportunity.) Collect all the secrets and type them into a word processor, using appropriate text styles and (possibly) clip art, to produce a page from the ancients' 'Book of Secrets'.

Worksheet 8 – How Red Wolf Escaped

Task:

Writing a report, explaining how Red Wolf escaped.

Support:

First, make sure that pupils are aware of the series of events that led to Red Wolf's escape.

Discuss Police Chief Hancuff's approach to the report that he must write. How is he going to make it clear that, whatever happened, it wasn't his fault? Come up with a good list of excuses.

Include in the Word box any further words arising out of the discussion.

Extension:

Police Chief Hancuff's boss is not impressed! Write his reply.

BOFFIN BOY'S PAL IS A CROOK

Word box

- Ninja
- gang
- CCTV
- gold bars
- dangerous
- surprised
- truck
- hold-up
- gunpoint
- police

Police Chief Hancuff was sure Wu Pee was a crook, but I was sure he wasn't!

I think Wu Pee is a crook because

I'm sure he isn't because

Worksheet 3: Boffin Boy's Plan

Boffin Boy came up with a clever plan to find out what Wu Pee was up to! I wish he wouldn't do these dangerous things …

This is my plan, Mum! First I'll

Then

I'm worried that

Worksheet 4: Wu Pee's Forest of the Ninja Quiz

Try to answer these questions! If you get them all right, the wonderful prize is … er … ask your teacher!

1. What does CCTV stand for?

C……………………… C……………………. T …………………………

2. Who is the most feared of all the Ninja?

3. Why wasn't I pleased to see Boffin Boy?

4. Why did the Ninja test the gold bars with a magnet?

5. What horrible death would I suffer if I didn't kill Boffin Boy?

6. Why did I pretend to be a crook?

7. How did Boffin Boy's Death Pills work?

8. So who wrote 'Romeo and Juliet'?

W……………………… S………………………………

9. What was the password to open the door?

10. What amazing secret did I find in the books of the ancients?

These mixed up words are called anagrams. They all come from the story! Can you work out what each one says? I've given you some clues.

Here's how anagrams work. If you move these letters around – rokoC – you get the word 'Crook'.

I've given you a bit of extra help – the capital letter is always the first letter of the word you're looking for.

Here's an easy one to start you off:

Peu eW _ _ _ _ _

BoBoniffy _ _ _ _ _ _ _ _ _ _ (Clue – our hero!)

setorF _ _ _ _ _ _ (Clue – where it all happened.)

wassProd _ _ _ _ _ _ _ _ (Clue – useful for getting in.)

reStsec _ _ _ _ _ _ _ (Clue – I'm always looking for these.)

hateDlliP _ _ _ _ _ _ _ _ _ (Boffin Boy's clever trick – pity Red Wolf found out about it!)

WoRdelf _ _ _ _ _ _ _ (Clue – what a villain!)

oomeR dAn lieJut _ _ _ _ _ _ _ _ _ _ _ _ _ _ (Clue – they came to a sad end, but not in our story.)

acEsped _ _ _ _ _ _ _ (Clue – What WORDELF did in the end.)

aNswerpep _ _ _ _ _ _ _ _ _ (Clue – How Boffin Boy found out that Wu Pee was a 'crook'.)

bInisevil _ _ _ _ _ _ _ _ _ (Clue: Ninja can make themselves this – or can they?)

Romeo and Juliet is my favourite play by Shakespeare. This is what happens.

Romeo and Juliet are in love, but Juliet's parents don't want her to marry him. They can't stand his family.

Her friend comes up with a plan. He gives her a death pill, just like the one I invented. When she swallows it, her family think she's dead, so they put her in the family tomb.

This is the bit where the plan goes a bit wrong. Someone is meant to tell Romeo what's going on, but this doesn't happen. He finds out that Juliet is dead (though we know she isn't, really). So he goes to her tomb just to check.

When he gets there, he finds

He is so upset, he

Then the death pill wears off, and Juliet wakes up.
She finds

She's really, really upset, so she

So, in the end, the two families

FROM THE SECRET BOOKS OF THE ANCIENTS.

SECRET 1 – How to make people think you are really brainy.

How to do it …

SECRET 2 – How to move from one place to another, really fast.

How to do it …

SECRET 3 – How to get out of trouble if you haven't done your homework.

How to do it …

SECRET 4 – ……………………………………………………………………………

How to do it …

Worksheet 8: How Red Wolf Escaped

I was in big trouble when Red Wolf escaped! I had to write a report for my boss, explaining how it happened …

Word box

- Death pill
- Boffin Boy
- thought
- alive
- sneaked

Dear Boss,

The first thing I have to say is that, whatever anyone says, it wasn't my fault.

After all, capturing Red Wolf was very brave and clever, wasn't it?

The trouble was ______________________________

Worksheet 1 – Snugbite's Story

Task:

Retelling the narrative from the point of view of the second Snurgon.

Support:

The activity is supported by sentence starters. For a more challenging activity, these starters could be reduced to fewer words, or even removed.

If necessary, supply a list of useful words, or work with pupils to build a word list from the text.

Extension:

Snugbite is going to write a postcard home – write the postcard for him. This is a précis exercise in reducing the story to around 50 words.

Worksheet 2 – Not Getting Lost

Task:

Instruction text: ways of avoiding being lost in a maze of caves.

Support:

Discuss with pupils how the various items could be used to help – i.e. tying the end of the string to the entrance to the cave, marking the route taken with paint, and drawing a map en route.

The writing, though simple, should take the form of a sequential instructional text, starting with a 'what you need' heading.

Extension:

Pupils could come up with alternative ideas for avoiding getting lost.

The instructional text could form the basis of story writing, perhaps with a different setting.

Worksheet 3 – Why Isn't Pluto a Planet?

Task:

Working a set of muddled notes up into continuous prose, in the form of a email.

Support:

The reasons for Pluto's demotion from planet status are not completely straight-forward: it's relatively small size is only one factor. Pupils may like to add to the information provided by Professor Mudweed by researching the topic on the Internet.

Extension:

The information on Pluto could form the basis of further research/extended writing on dwarf planets and other Kuiper Belt objects.

Worksheet 4 – Wu Pee's Quiz

Task:

Creating thought bubbles for Wu Pee, to comment on the action of the story.

Support:

Filling in the thought bubbles will require close reading of the text. Ask pupils to do this, making notes as they go along, before filling in their ideas on the worksheet.

The thoughts should be written in the first person.

Extension:

Use the information for a piece of continuous writing, in which Wu Pee sends his thoughts in a letter to a friend.

Worksheet 5 – Glossary

Task:

Create a glossary for words in the text.

Support:

Some of the words to be glossed may need research – e.g. moon, Pluto, Charon. Encourage pupils to extend their definitions with additional key facts.

Some entries (e.g. door-opening twiddly thing) require a more imaginative approach.

Extension:

ICT opportunity: use the definitions for a picture dictionary entry or article for Boffin Boy's on-line encyclopaedia Boffipedia, finding appropriate clip art and extending the definitions.

Worksheet 6 – Boffin Boy's Door-opening Twiddly Thing

Task:

Writing an explanatory text.

Support:

Remind pupils that Red Wolf is an arch-villain, for whom a device to open doors would be really useful! The sheet should be used to explain how Red Wolf put the gadget to various nefarious uses.

Extension:

Expand the notes into a new Boffin Boy/Red Wolf adventure, either in continuous text or designed as a graphic novel.

Worksheet 7 – Word Mazes

Task:

Solving word mazes.

Support:

Explain that the object is to work through the maze, writing down the numbers in the correct order, as each number is reached. The key can then be used to create a sentence.

Note: not all the words included in the key actually appear in the word mazes.

The completed sentences are:

- Grizbold is on Pluto in the Snurgon space ship.
- Boffin Boy and Wu Pee are lost in the ice caves.
- You need woolly space socks in the snow on Pluto.

Extension:

Use further copies of the maze (photocopied as necessary) to send further coded messages.

Worksheet 8 – Planning Another Adventure

Task:

Story planning.

Support:

The sheet provides scaffolding for a further interplanetary Boffin Boy story. When pupils have decided on which planet (or moon) to locate their story, encourage them to research details on conditions there, which can then be woven into the narrative.

Extension:

Pupils should now write the story, in prose or graphic novel form.

Worksheet 1: Snugbite's Story

Grizbold and I went to Pluto to ....

....

....

While we were there, our spaceship ....

....

....

We thought we might ....

....

Luckily, two characters arrived called ....

....

....

Grizbold told me that. ....

....

....

We tried to get out of the ice caves, but ....

....

....

At last we got out, but there was another problem ....

....

Luckily for us. ....

....

....

....

In the end ....

....

....

This is the part of the story where we got lost in the ice caves. Boffin Boy said he knew the way out, but he didn't! These pictures show three things that could have helped us. Can you explain how we could have used them?

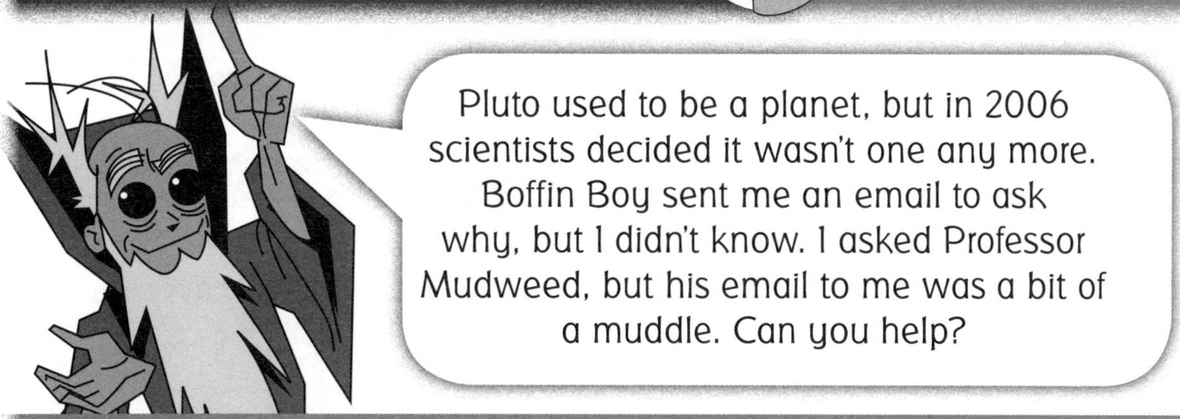

From: mail@mudweed.com

To: wupee@ninjamail.wiz

Too small. 2360 in diameter. Lots of moons bigger than that.
Other objects we've found are bigger than Pluto. Real planets orbit the sun in a circle. Pluto has an egg-shaped orbit ...
...now called a dwarf planet.

From wupee@ninjamail.wiz

To: boffinboy@boffinboy.com

Hi Boffin Boy,
I got an email about Pluto from Professor Mudweed, but it was a muddle.
So I've had to sort it out!

Scientists have decided that Pluto isn't a planet any more because

Can you guess what I was thinking at these points in the story?

1. When we got to Pluto.

2. When we went outside the spaceship.

3. When Boffin Boy found something under the great pile of snow.

4. When we got lost in the ice caves.

5. When we came out of the ice caves.

6. When we couldn't get in to Boffin Boy's space ship.

7. When we were ready to go home.

Glossary

alien	
Charon	
Door-opening twiddly thing	
hibernation	
moon	
Pluto	
Snurgon	
space socks	
superhero	
universe	
Wizard	

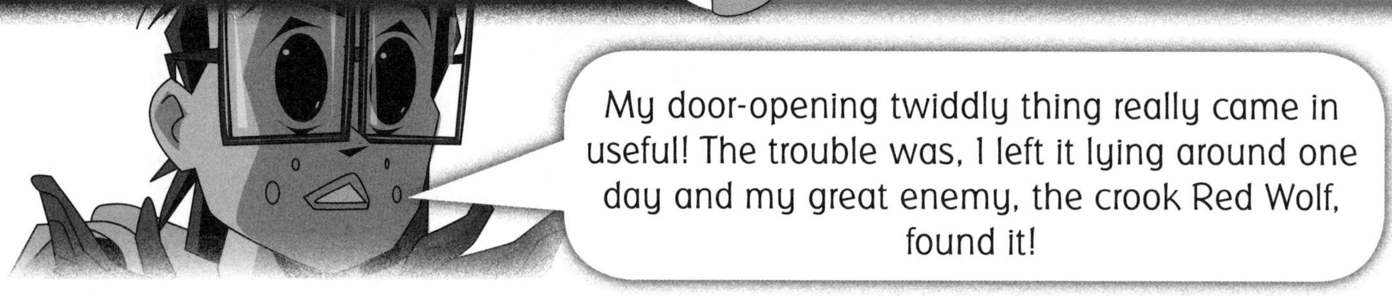

What do you think he might have done with it?

1 Red Wolf …

2 Red Wolf …

3 Red Wolf …

These word mazes are great! Find your way through the maze and make a list of the numbers in the right order. Then work out what the message says!

1) ice caves 2) space ship 3) Snurgon 4) is 5) Wu Pee 6) Grizbold 7) Pluto 8) the 9) lost 10) you 11) moon 12) snow 13) frozen 14) on 15) near 16) water 17) woolly space socks 18) by 19) need 20) in 21) space 22) Boffin Boy 23) and 24) next 25) are

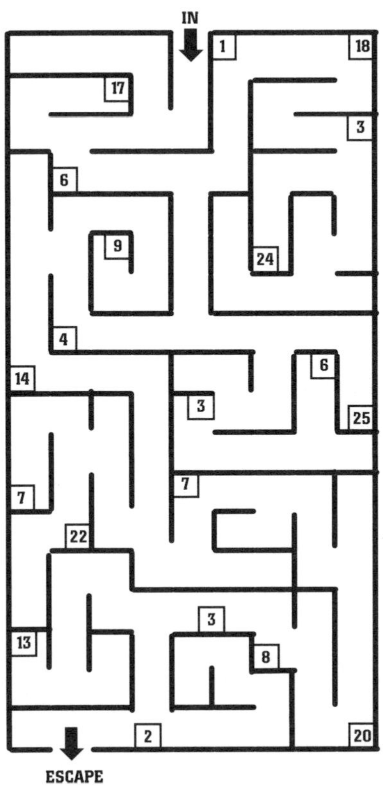

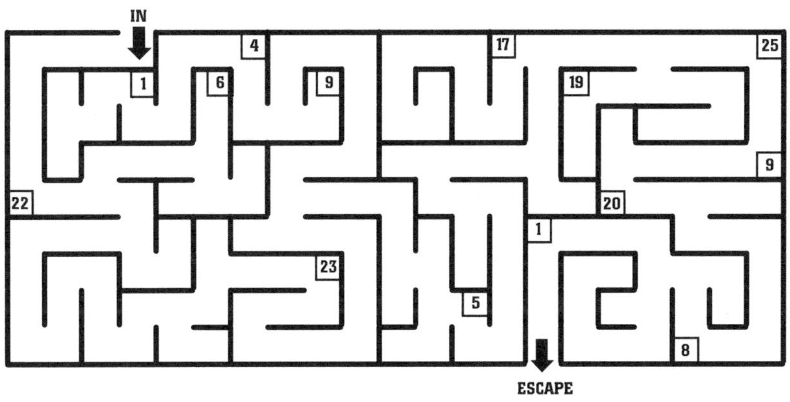

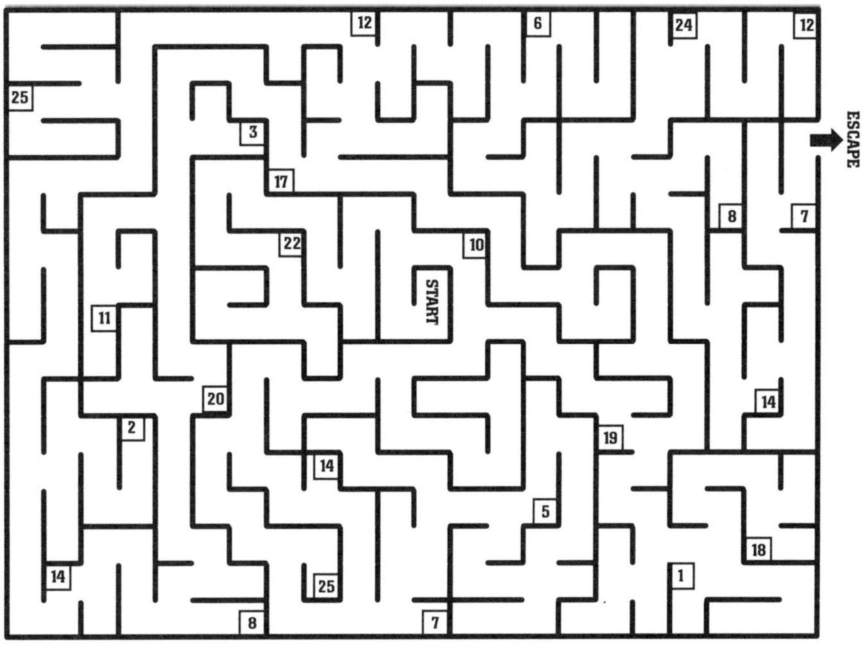

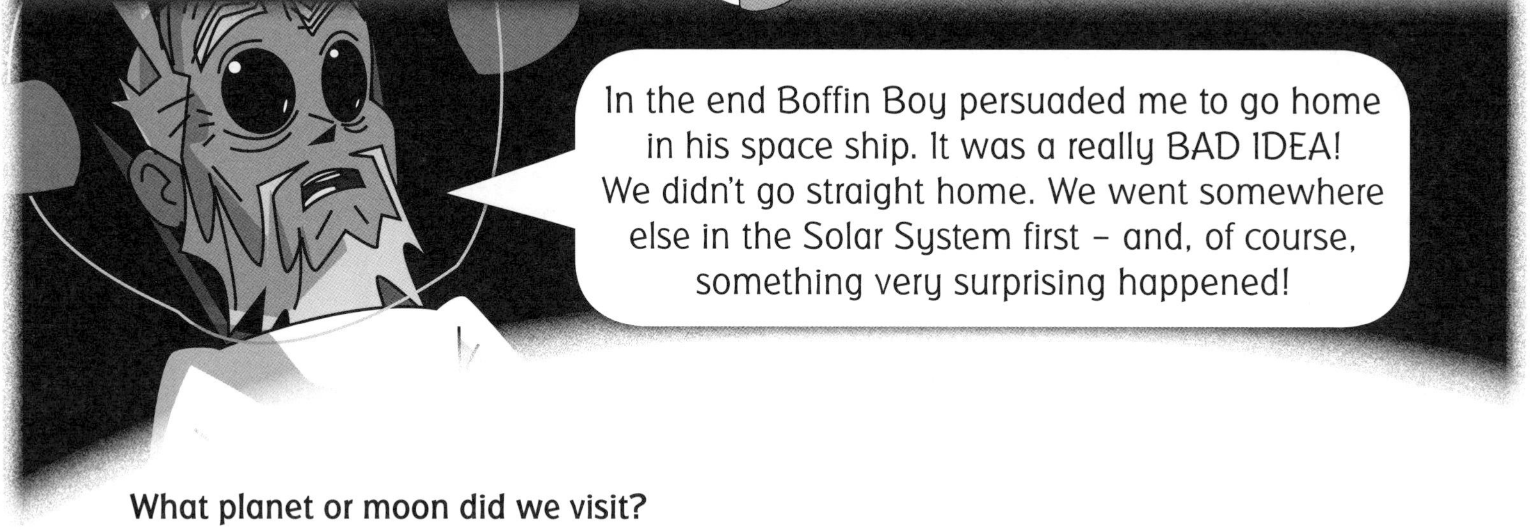

What planet or moon did we visit?

What did we find there?

Was it a good or bad situation?

What did Boffin Boy do?

What did I do to help?

How was it sorted out in the end?

Worksheet 1 – TV Report

Task:

Write a TV interview in the form of a script.

Support:

Role-play the activity first. Explain that the TV interviewer will probably be asking for more gruesome detail than Hancuff is prepared to give. How does he deal with this? What awkward questions might the interviewer ask – e.g. 'Why haven't you solved it yet?'

Ensure that pupils are familiar with the conventions of script writing.

Extension:

Write a second interview, which takes place at the end of the story. This can be with any of the key characters.

Worksheet 2 – Retelling the Story

Task:

A first person narrative, retelling the story from the point of view of Chika.

Support:

Ensure that pupils are clear on the events of the narrative. If necessary, help by working on a list of bullet points first. More able pupils can extend the narrative into a diary, with additional ideas of their own. Less able pupils can simply complete the sentences.

Extension:

A year later, the killer bugs strike again! Write the entry for Chika's diary for this point in time. This could be extended into story writing.

Worksheet 3 – Killer Bugs Website

Task:

Design a web page using information from the text.

Support:

Work through the four headings on the copy master, listing key facts. In particular, focus on writing a strong introductory sentence. What should this contain? (Examples: a powerful warning, a reminder of the news story, etc.)

Decide on an appropriate illustration, which can be redrawn from the text.

Extension:

Use the same format to research and write about other insects – e.g. garden pests, or insects with harmful bites.

Worksheet 4 – Word Code

Task:

Solving a letter substitution code.

Support:

Explain how a letter substitution code works. For more able pupil, the key could be blanked before copying and fewer letter codes could be given.

Missing letters: E = 14 S = 10

Extension:

Further work on word codes: pupils could design their own code sentences, or even simple grids, for others to solve.

Worksheet 5 – The Corpse's Story

Task:

Imaginative first person writing, using the events of the story as a starting point.

Support:

Brainstorm a range of possibilities for this story. Explain that 'the killer bugs killed me and took me to the cave' does not make a story. Ask questions, such as

- How did the corpse first become aware of the killer bugs?
- What did he think at first?

- How did he try to avoid them/escape from them?
- What warning might he give others?

Use the replies to add further words to the Word box.

Extension:

Write a narrative, as if written by someone who managed to escape from the killer bugs. How was this achieved? (The story can be as outrageous/silly as is wished.)

Worksheet 6 – A Poster

Task:

Design a poster for Professor Mudweed's bug killer.

Support:

Ask pupils to work in groups to make notes on the 'what to include' list on the Worksheet. What slogan would be effective in selling the product? The sheet can be used for a draft design, to be worked up later on a larger sheet of paper.

Extension:

Use the material produced to plan and script a TV advert.

Worksheet 7 – Bubbles

Task:

To create speech and thought bubbles for the given page.

Support:

Ensure that pupils are aware of the development of the narrative up to this point. Discuss, perhaps using role play, what Boffin Boy and Chika are likely to be saying to each other in the picture.

What might the killer bug be thinking? Run a competition for the funniest 'thought'.

Extension:

Write the same scene using direct speech, extending it if appropriate.

Worksheet 8 – Wu Pee to the Rescue

Task:

First person explanatory writing.

Support:

Make a list of the reasons why Wu Pee might have changed his mind about helping Boffin Boy – e.g. guilt at letting down his friend, realisation of the danger (how did Wu Pee find out about this?), or curiosity. Encourage pupils to consider that Wu Pee may have had more than one reason.

Extension:

Write an extra scene, perhaps in play script form, in which Wu Pee visits Professor Mudweed for advice.

When the TV news heard about what happened to Mrs Wiggins, they wanted to interview me! I wanted people (especially Boffin Boy) to know about the killer bugs, so they could help the police. But I didn't want to tell them all the horrible details! Can you write the interview?

TV Interviewer
Police Chief Hancuff, can you tell us what happened here?

P C Hancuff

TV Interviewer

P C Hancuff

TV Interviewer

P C Hancuff

TV Interviewer

P C Hancuff

TV Interviewer

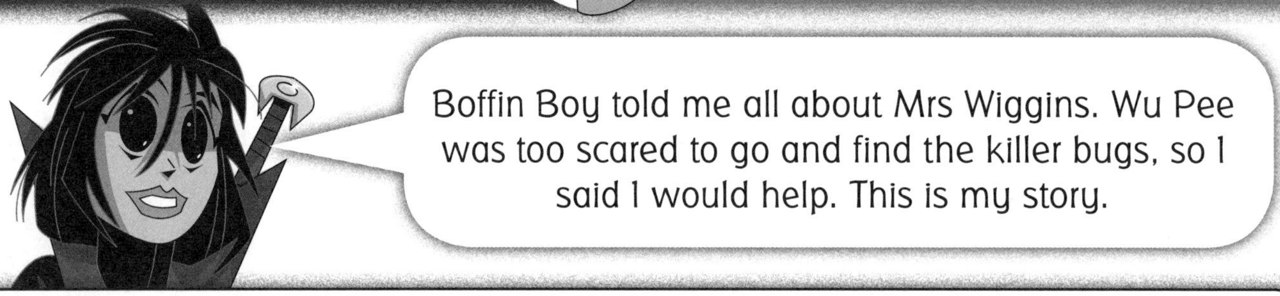

First we went to Mrs Wiggins' garden. We saw

When we got to the volcano

Inside the volcano, we found

Boffin Boy thought that

The bugs started hatching. We tried to escape, but

The bugs caught us and

Luckily for us

KILLER BUGS

Introduction

What we know about the killer bugs

Why we think they have woken up now

Why they are dangerous

Can you crack this word code? Most of the words are insects.
One word tells you what to say when a killer bug attacks you.
Another word says which bit of you they attack first.

4	14	14	1	11	14		12
14		9		5			7
14	9	7		6		16	8
		17	9	10	13		12
		8		14			3
4	6	2	10				14
				2	15	9	1

Key: 1 = T 2 = G 3 = K 4 = B 5 = O 6 = U 7 = R 8 = I 9 = A 10 = ?
11 = L 12 = C 13 = P 14 = ? 15 = N 16 = H 17 = W 18 = D 19 = Y

Now crack this sentence:

17	9	1	12	16	5	6	1	
1	16	14	7	14	10	9		
3	8	11	11	14	7	4	6	2
4	14	16	8	15	18	19	5	6

I guess you're wondering how the killer bugs got me! Well, it happened like this ...

I was out for a nice country walk, just minding my own business, when

Useful words

noise attack
swarm
poison
flew
carried
sticky
strong
starve

Me again. I had this brilliant idea to make a load of cash selling my extra-strong bug killer, called MUDDO. I need a poster, but I'm rubbish at posters – can you help?

What to include:

Picture of the product	Why it is brilliant at killing bugs	What Wu Pee says about it	How to buy it

This picture doesn't have any speech or thought bubbles. Can you write some?

At first, Wu Pee wouldn't help me deal with the killer bugs. But in the end, he saved us! I wonder why he changed his mind?

When Boffin Boy told me about the killer bugs, I

When I thought about it later, I

The following five picture resource pages are provided to enable pupils to undertake a variety of tasks in a more creative way.

The following are merely some starting point suggestions for their use:

1. Cut out appropriate pictures of the villains. Create 'Wanted Posters'.
2. Design appropriate backgrounds for one of the stories from the books, or for a new story. Then cut out appropriate characters to illustrate a scene from the book or story.
3. Use the characters, objects and speech / thought bubbles to mock up a page using the graphic novel style.
4. Discuss possible alternative endings for stories, and continue the story in graphic novel format.
5. Develop a board game based on one of the books. Use the characters to produce cards. Create further cards to illustrate weapons.
6. Create puzzles in the same styles as those in the workbooks – word searches, codes, etc.
7. Devise maps for various locations described in the books. Illustrate with appropriate characters.
8. Use as illustrations for pupils' own stories.
9. Design Web pages, perhaps by scanning the images and using them in an appropriate design program.

Graphic Novels and ICT

Microsoft Word provides facilities for pupils to design their own graphic novel pages. Objects such as clip art or pupils' own scanned pictures can be imported into the page.

A range of callouts (speech and thought bubbles) are included in Microsoft Word, and can be pasted in. To find them, open the Drawing toolbar, click on Autoshapes then Callouts. Text can then be placed in the callouts, which can be dragged into position.

In addition, the Drawing toolbar offers a Word Art feature ideal for 'sound effect' words such as 'Kaboom!' Text boxes can be used for caption boxes in the pages, and both text boxes and the callouts can have colour fills.

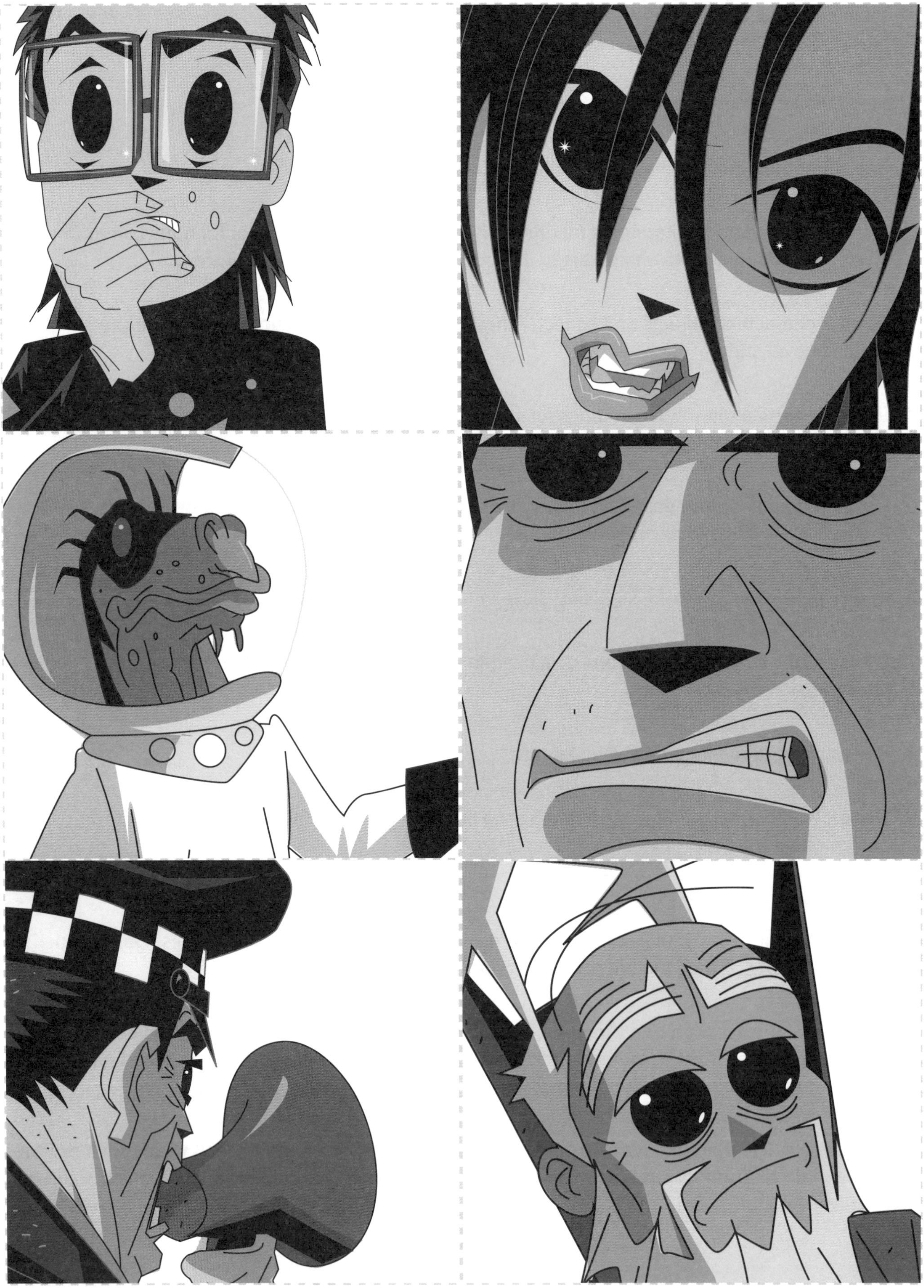

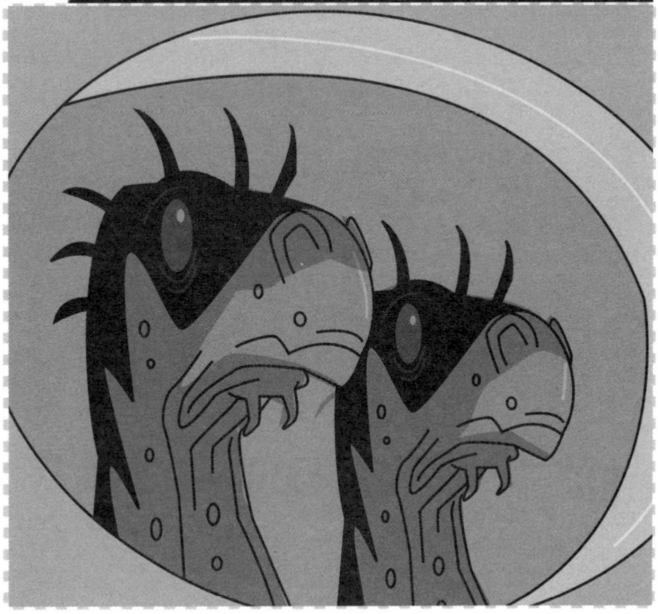

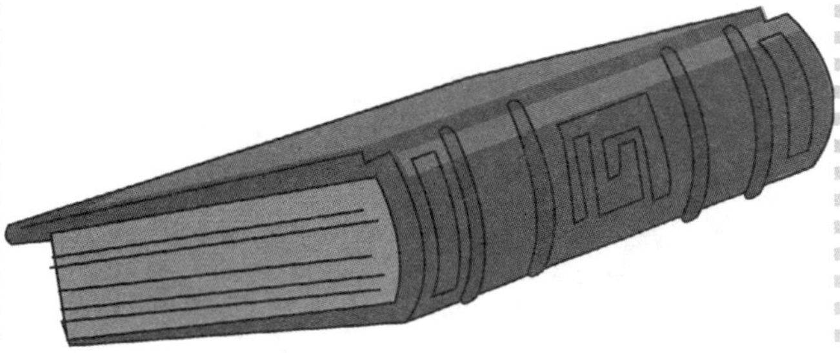

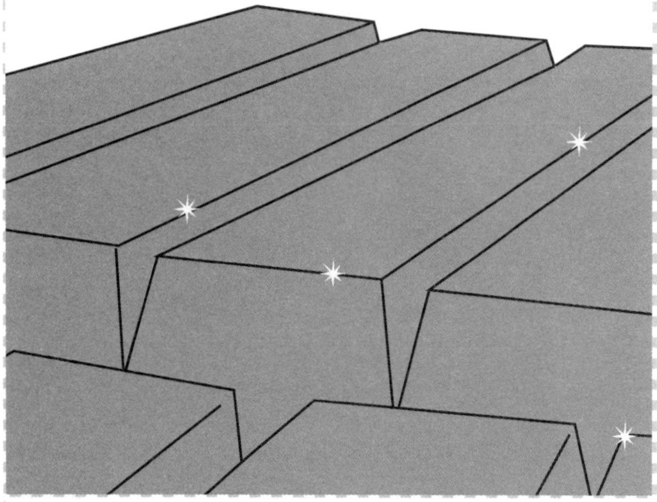

BUG SPRAY

Callouts